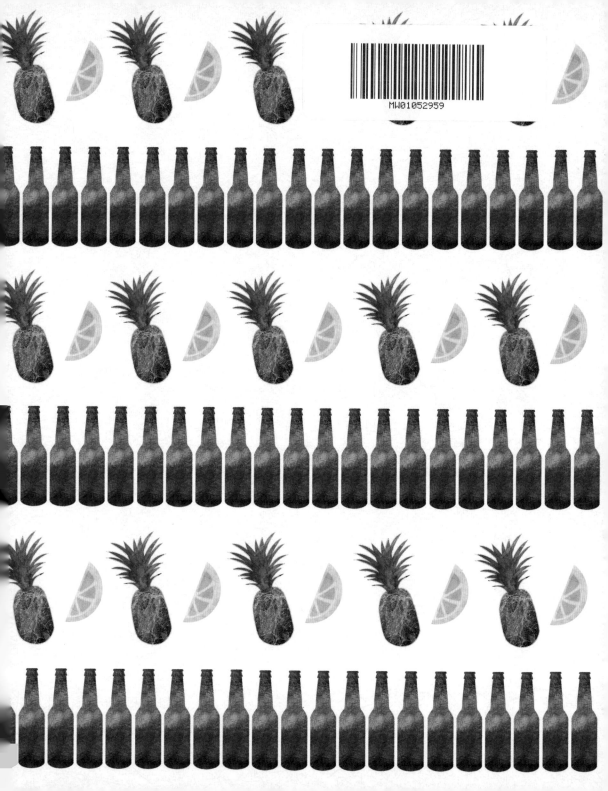

Beer Cocktails

Smith Street Books

DAVE ADAMS

Contents

The Wonderful
World of Beer 5

Lagers

Pales & Ales

Saisons, Sours, Weizens & Wildcards

Stouts, Porters & Other Dark Beers

The Wonderful World of Beer

I love drinking beer. I love the way it looks, I love the way it smells, I love the way it tastes, I love the way it feels in my mouth. I love the smell of a brewery when it is malting grain. Above all, I love the way it makes me feel. It is a drink for all occasions. There are so many different varieties of beer that you can always find one to suit the mood you're in. There are so many flavours that you can also find a beer to suit anyone's palate. There are so many colours, you can even find one to match your outfit.

Not everyone thinks they like beer. I get that. Your first beer was probably a terrible, watery, mass-produced lager with no discernible flavour or identity. I don't like those beers either, but there are so many other styles you can try. Beer has a very grown-up flavour: it is bitter. While bitterness can take some time to get used to, it can be a truly fantastic element of flavour. Bitterness can counteract fattiness in food, it can refresh your palate, and bitter foods and drinks can aid digestion.

This book is a gateway into the wonderful world of beer. For those who already love beer and can't get enough of the stuff, and for those who think they are indifferent to its charms. By using beer as a cocktail ingredient, you can appreciate the different flavours and characteristics it offers, without having to drink an entire pint of the stuff. Who knows, after all this experimentation, you might even find a beer you like!

Different Types of Beer

There are so many different styles of beer, with brewers coming up with new ones all the time. They can vary wildly, from bitter floral hoppiness to sweet biscuity maltiness; from high-alcohol sippers to low-alcohol sessionable ales; big, dark smoky beers to light, crisp clear ones – as well as everything in between. Here is a basic overview of some of the major beer categories.

LAGER

Lager is the term for beer that is fermented at a lower temperature. They're often quite clear, crisp and lightly hopped. There should be some bitterness in the drink from the hops, without being overpoweringly bitter. There are plenty of good lagers in the world, but unfortunately, there are more terrible ones – often sold in tall, see-through bottles.

DARK LAGER

This is beer that is cold fermented, but using toasted, darker malts. This process imparts colour and flavour into the beer. Dark lagers can range from caramelly, full-bodied amber beers, all the way through to smoky, chocolatey black beers.

PALE ALE

'Pale ale' can technically mean many different things. While it sounds like it's referrring just to the appearance of the beer, generally speaking, if you see 'pale ale' on a beer label these days, it means that it has been made in the American style, with up-front floral fruitiness with a light bitterness on the finish. Despite the name, they can sometimes be quite amber in colour.

IPA

'India pale ale' is not from India. It was created in England to last the long voyage at sea to get to India. It was made with higher alcohol and a shirt-load of hops to act as a preservative. It is very bitter and probably not great for a first-time beer drinker, but it's very rewarding once you've acquired the taste.

SAISON

Saison is a style of beer created by the Belgians. Traditionally, it was a low-alcohol farmhouse ale made for the workers using all the leftover grains and hops from the proper brew. As with most old-fashioned peasant food, it has been perfected over the years, and is now one of the most versatile beer styles around. Because of the mish-mash of ingredients, the flavours of saison can vary infinitely and the opportunities for brewers to interpret the style are almost endless. Experiment with different ones to find your favourite.

WHEAT BEER

Wheat beer is made from – you guessed it – wheat, instead of barley. Pale in colour, and often lower in alcohol, wheat beer has a distinct mouthfeel and a light, fruity flavour. Sometimes wheat beer is flavoured with cloves, orange rind or even coriander (cilantro). There are many different names for wheat beer. Witbier, hefeweizen and weissbier are all different words for different styles of wheat beer. *Weizen* is German for 'wheat', and *hefe* means 'yeast'. Therefore, *hefeweizen* is a wheat beer that has been bottle conditioned and contains some yeast sediment.

The Germans also have kristallweizen, which is a clear wheat beer and dunkelweizen which is dark wheat beer. There is also *witbier* or *weissbier* which translates to 'white beer'. These are your standard wheat beers from the Netherlands, Belgium and Germany. The French call it La Biere Blanche.

BROWN ALE

Brown ales are usually more malt-driven than pale ales. This lends the beer nutty, caramelly characteristics, with less bitterness and more sweetness.

PORTER

This is a black beer made from dark, toasted malt, but usually without the burnt bitterness of a stout. Porters can often be quite sweet, with rich flavours of coffee and chocolate.

STOUT

Similar to porter, but generally not as sweet, stouts can vary in style greatly. Irish stout, such as Guinness, tends to be gassed with nitrogen instead of carbon dioxide, giving a beer with smaller bubbles and a creamy head. Milk stout has lactose sugar added, to impart a sweet caramel flavour. Oatmeal stout has a smooth mouthfeel and a lingering sweetness. There is a whole world to explore with stouts.

BELGIAN ALES

The Belgians are the masters of brewing. The Trappist monks have been doing it for a thousand years. Belgian ales range in style from the lighter, malty blonde ales, all the way to the high-alcohol dark ales. Belgian beers are very traditional and stay true to their style, so you won't find a lot of up-front floral hoppiness as you do with some modern beers.

SOURS & LAMBICS

Now we're getting in the really whacky category. These are my personal favourites. Sour beers often use wild yeast and open-vat fermentation, creating very unusual flavours that sometimes make you question whether you're drinking a beer at all. You will often find sour beers flavoured with fruit such as raspberries and strawberries, making them particularly great for cocktail experimentation.

OPTIMAL SERVING TEMPERATURES

There is much debate about what temperature different beers should be served at. In Australia, beer is served as cold as possible. In the UK, ales are served at room temperature. The warmer the beer, the more you can taste the flavours. Ultimately it is up to the drinker. For the cocktails in this book, I would suggest everything is served as cold as possible. It's easier to let a drink warm up than it is to chill it back down.

TO MAKE SUGAR SYRUP

Bring 220 g (8 oz/1 cup) sugar and 250 ml (8½ fl oz) water to the boil in a saucepan over medium–high heat, stirring occasionally. Reduce the heat to low and simmer for 10–15 minutes, or until the mixture reaches a syrupy consistency. Allow to cool, then transfer to a clean sealable bottle or jar. The sugar syrup will keep in the fridge for 2 weeks.

Now that you've had a brief introduction to the wonderful and vast world of beer, I'm sure you're desperate for a tasty beverage to quench your insatiable thirst.

Lagers

Shandy

Shandy is sweet and innocent. She's great to have at lunchtime on a hot day when you've still got work to do. Traditionally made with lager, she can be beefed up by using stronger-flavoured beer like an American pale ale.

SERVES 1

45 ml (1½ fl oz) sugar syrup (page 9)

45 ml (1½ fl oz) freshly squeezed lemon juice

45 ml (1½ fl oz) chilled soda water (seltzer)

140 ml (4½ fl oz) lager or lightly hopped pale ale

lemon wheel and mint sprig, to garnish

Combine the sugar syrup, lemon juice and soda water in a chilled beer glass.

Top up with the beer.

Garnish with a lemon wheel and a sprig of mint.

Fluttering Shandy

Agave nectar liqueur is like cordial for adults. It has a delicious, unique flavour that is a lot more interesting than your traditional lemon or lime cordial. Try this recipe with lighter-tasting beers such as lager or Pacific ale.

SERVES 1

45 ml (1½ fl oz) agave nectar liqueur

330 ml (11 fl oz) bottle lager or Pacific ale

lime, to garnish

Pour the agave liqueur into a tall glass filled with ice.

Top with the beer and garnish with lime.

Hop, Skip & Go Naked

When Shandy grew up, she went to college and really let her hair down. Her parents must be so proud.

SERVES 20–30

700 ml (23½ fl oz) bottle vodka
500 ml (17 fl oz) freshly squeezed lemon juice
500 ml (17 fl oz) grenadine
24 x 330 ml (11 fl oz) cans mass-produced American lager

In a chilled, completely clean bathtub, combine all the ingredients.

Garnish with a bikini top.

Respect one another.

Steam Roller

Steam ale is an American style of beer, and some would say it kickstarted the craft beer renaissance that has made the modern world such a wonderful place. Effectively, it uses lager yeast but ferments at ale temperatures, giving us a beer that is sessionable like a lager, but full bodied like an ale.

SERVES 1

30 ml (1 fl oz) elderflower liqueur

15 ml (½ fl oz) cherry liqueur

30 ml (1 fl oz) rye whiskey

30 ml (1 fl oz) freshly squeezed lemon juice

330 ml (11 fl oz) bottle steam ale

lemon twist, to garnish

In a cocktail shaker filled with ice, combine the liqueurs, whiskey and lemon juice. Shake vigorously.

Strain into a chilled pint glass. Carefully top up with beer.

Garnish with a twist of lemon rind.

El Ayudacal

There are many, many ways to make tasteless Mexican beers not so tasteless, but still keeping them Mexican. Here is one such cocktail.

SERVES 1

45 ml (1½ fl oz) lime juice, freshly squeezed
1 lime, zested
20 ml (¾ fl oz) agave nectar
330 ml (11 fl oz) bottle Mexican lager
lime wedge, to garnish

In a chilled beer glass, combine the lime juice, zest and agave with ice.

Slowly pour beer into the glass, being careful not to froth the beer too much.

Garnish with lime.

Raspberry Beeret

If The Artist Formerly Known as Prince drank cocktails, he probably would have drunk this cocktail.

---

1 cup (125 g/4½ oz) fresh raspberries, plus extra to garnish

---

120 ml (4 fl oz) vodka

1.25 litres (42 fl oz) raspberry lemonade

---

4 x 330 ml (11 fl oz) bottles lager

---

lime, to garnish

Lightly muddle the raspberries and vodka in a large jug or punch bowl.

Add 3 cups of ice and the lemonade.

Slowly add the beer and gently stir.

Pour into small cups filled with ice and garnish with lime and extra raspberries.

Hot
Michelada

You know those friends who come over and leave
a bottle of flavourless Mexican beer in your
fridge? Here's a drink that can put that *pißwasser*
to good use. There are many variations of the
michelada, and this is definitely one of them.

SERVES 2

1 tablespoon honey
3 tablespoons salt, plus a pinch extra
½ teaspoon smoked paprika
pinch of chilli powder
30 ml (1 fl oz) freshly squeezed lime juice
15 ml (½ fl oz) worcestershire sauce
10 ml (¼ fl oz) hot sauce (or more, to taste)
pinch of salt, extra
330 ml (11 fl oz) Mexican lager
freshly ground black pepper and pickled chilli, to garnish

Spread the honey on a plate and dip the rims of two chilled beer goblets in it.

On a separate plate, combine the salt, paprika and chilli powder.

Dip the honeyed glass rims into the salt mix.

Combine the lime juice, sauces and a pinch of salt in a cocktail shaker filled with ice and shake.

Strain into the goblets and add fresh ice.

Top with the beer. Add a sprinkling of black pepper and garnish each with pickled chilli.

Bloody Michelada

Here's a michelada you can enjoy with breakfast. You could also add a little vodka, if you're a high-functioning alcoholic like me.

1 lime, zested and quartered,
plus extra to garnish

1 tablespoon salt

1 teaspoon smoked paprika

5 coriander (cilantro) sprigs, chopped

20 ml (¾ fl oz) freshly squeezed lime juice

10 ml (¼ fl oz) freshly squeezed lemon juice

90 ml (3 fl oz) tomato juice

10 ml (¼ fl oz) hot sauce

330 ml (11 fl oz) Mexican lager

Run a lime quarter around the
rim of a large beer goblet.

On a plate, combine the salt,
lime zest and paprika.

Dip the rim of the goblet in the salt mix.

Combine the coriander, lime juice and lemon
juice in a cocktail shaker filled with ice. Shake
vigorously, then double strain into the goblet.

Add the tomato juice, hot sauce and a pinch
of salt. Stir to combine, then top with ice.

Upend the bottle of beer into the
glass and garnish with lime.

Beergarita

This cocktail takes your favourite flavourless Mexican lager and hides it in one of Mexico's most famous salty–sour drinks. Be careful with this one. It contains all of the alcohol of a margarita, with the sessionability of an icy cold beer.

SERVES 1

salt, for rimming
60 ml (2 fl oz) tequila
30 ml (1 fl oz) triple sec
30 ml (1 fl oz) freshly squeezed lime juice
10 ml (¼ fl oz) lime cordial
330 ml (11 fl oz) bottle Mexican lager
lime, to garnish

In a chilled, salt rimmed pint glass, combine the tequila, triple sec, lime juice and cordial. Fill with ice.

Upend the bottle of beer into the glass.

Garnish with lime.

Danza de la Cerveza

This little dance for two is full of passion, lust and tequila. Is there anything more romantic that staring into each other's eyes across a frozen sea of alcohol with beer bottles floating in it? Not that I'm aware of. It's like *Lady and the Tramp*, but made with real tramps.

SERVES 2

90 ml (3 fl oz) tequila
45 ml (1½ fl oz) triple sec
60 ml (2 fl oz) lemon juice
30 ml (1 fl oz) lime cordial
salt, for rimming
2 x 330 ml (11 fl oz) bottles Mexican lager
lemon, to garnish

Combine the tequila, triple sec, lemon juice
and cordial in a blender with 2 cups ice.

Blend at high speed until smooth.

Pour into a very large margarita
glass rimmed with salt.

Upend both opened beer bottles into
the margarita, garnish with lemon
and let the fireworks begin.

Cerveza Nicola

Imagine sitting on a beach in Sardinia on a sunny afternoon, the crystal turquoise waters of the Mediterranean lapping your toes, the salty breeze on your skin, your belly content with fresh pasta. What else could one possibly want? Only this drink.

SERVES 1

20 ml (¾ fl oz) Campari
20 ml (¾ fl oz) vodka
330 ml (11 fl oz) bottle Italian lager
orange, to garnish

In a tall, chilled glass filled with ice, combine the Campari and vodka.

Carefully add the beer.

Garnish with orange and forget all your cares.

Captain's Keg

This summery beer cocktail works best with lighter-flavoured beers, such as an Australian pilsner. It will also ensure you don't contract scurvy on those long voyages at sea.

SERVES 2

salt, for rimming
60 ml (2 fl oz) spiced rum
60 ml (2 fl oz) guava juice
60 ml (2 fl oz) freshly squeezed pink grapefruit juice
330 ml (11 fl oz) bottle pilsner
pink grapefruit, to garnish

Rim two chilled beer glasses with salt, then fill with ice.

Divide the rum, and guava and grapefruit juice between the two glasses and stir.

Carefully top up with beer. Garnish with grapefruit and make noises like a pirate.

Chelada

Clamato – clam broth, mixed with tomato juice – sounds like it ought to be disgusting. Turns out it's delicious, especially in Bloody Marys and oyster shooters. It can be a bit hard to find in some parts of the world, but track some down and chow down on this tasty clam chelada.

SERVES 1

salt, for rimming
180 ml (6 fl oz) lager
120 ml (4 fl oz) Clamato
20 ml (¾ fl oz) freshly squeezed lime juice
lime, to garnish

Rim a chilled pint glass with salt and fill with ice.

Add the beer, Clamato and lime juice and stir to combine.

Garnish with lime.

Vitamin C

Mass-produced American lager is, let's face it, not that great. This tonic makes up for all of its inadequacies, putting the colour, flavour and alcohol back into the beverage.

SERVES 2

60 ml (2 fl oz) gin
125 ml (4 fl oz) chilled freshly squeezed orange juice
330 ml (11 fl oz) bottle mass-produced American lager
orange, to garnish

Divide the gin and orange juice into two chilled beer glasses.

Carefully top up with the beer.

Garnish with orange.

Jamexican Bodega Cobbler

Equal parts Jamaican and Mexican,
this cobbled-together cocktail is a stunning
reminder that beautiful things can happen
when cultures intermingle.

SERVES 1

220 g (8 oz/1 cup) demerara sugar

30 ml (1 fl oz) Jamaican rum

1 orange slice

10 ml (¼ fl oz) freshly squeezed lemon juice

330 ml (11 fl oz) bottle Mexican lager

orange, lemon and mint, to garnish

Bring the sugar and 250 ml (8½ fl oz) water
to the boil in a saucepan over medium–
high heat, stirring occasionally.

Reduce the heat to low and simmer
for 10–15 minutes, or until the mixture
reaches a syrupy consistency.

Allow to cool, then transfer to a clean
sealable bottle or jar. The demerara syrup
will keep in the fridge for 2 weeks.

In a cocktail shaker filled with ice, combine 10 ml
(¼ fl oz) of the sugar syrup, the rum, orange
slice and lemon juice. Shake vigorously.

Strain into a chilled beer glass
filled with crushed ice.

Slowly add the beer, adding
more ice if necessary.

Garnish with orange, lemon and mint.

Redneck Mother

This little mother knows how to have a good time. She doesn't really like the taste of beer, but that's not going to stop her tonight. Just don't let her drive the house into a car again.

SERVES 2

60 ml (2 fl oz) sloe gin
60 ml (2 fl oz) grapefruit juice
330 ml (11 fl oz) bottle pale lager
330 ml (11 fl oz) bottle ginger beer
pink grapefruit, to garnish

Divide the gin and grapefruit juice between two tall beer glasses filled with ice. Stir to combine.

Slowly add the beer to each.

Top up with ginger beer and garnish with grapefruit.

French Monaco

A pink drink for when you want to look sophisticated, but when you'd still prefer to drink beer. You could sip this with your tennis partner down at the country club.

SERVES 2

60 ml (2 fl oz) pomegranate molasses

120 ml (4 fl oz) lemonade

330 ml (11 fl oz) bottle steam ale

lemon, to garnish

Divide the molasses and lemonade between two tall beer glasses filled with ice.

Slowly top up with beer.

Garnish with lemon.

Coupe de Ville

Here's a great boozy bowl of nonsense that will quickly use up that carton of Mexican lager your father-in-law gave you for Christmas last year. You might even put him to sleep with this baby too.

SERVES 6–12

180 ml (6 fl oz) tequila

90 ml (3 fl oz) Cointreau

180 ml (6 fl oz) freshly squeezed orange juice

180 ml (6 fl oz) freshly squeezed lime juice

6 x 330 ml (11 fl oz) bottles Mexican lager

orange, lemon and lime slices, to garnish

In a large punch bowl, combine the tequila, Cointreau, orange juice and lime juice.
Add some large blocks of ice and stir.

Carefully pour in the beer.

Garnish with lots of citrus slices.

Snake Bite

This cocktail is favoured by English backpackers in Irish bars all around the world. Strange thing is, I've never met one who can handle them – after the third one, they always turn into a right a-hole.

SERVES 1

250 ml (8½ fl oz) lager
250 ml (8½ fl oz) cider
30 ml (1 fl oz) blackcurrant cordial

In a chilled pint glass, combine all the ingredients.

Try not to hurt anyone.

Beerly Legal

This delightful drink is guaranteed to
make you feel young again.

SERVES 1

60 ml (2 fl oz) tangerine juice
30 ml (1 fl oz) Aperol
330 ml (11 fl oz) bottle lager
maraschino cherry, to garnish

Combine the tangerine juice and Aperol
in a pint glass filled with ice and stir.

Carefully top up with lager.

Garnish with a cherry and drink through those
curly straws that you wear as glasses.

Italian Stallion

Passionate, sexy, potent and sophisticated. These are all words people have used to describe me. Usually prefixed with *not very*, *definitely not*, *im-* and *un-*. This is why I drink.

2 fresh sage leaves
¼ ruby grapefruit, chopped
15 ml (½ fl oz) freshly squeezed lime juice
30 ml (1 fl oz) Campari
30 ml (1 fl oz) Aperol
15 ml (½ fl oz) sugar syrup (page 9)
45 ml (1½ fl oz) lager
grapefruit, to garnish

Muddle the sage and grapefruit in a cocktail shaker. Add the lime juice, Campari, Aperol and sugar syrup, along with 1 cup ice. Shake vigorously. Strain into a large old fashioned glass filled with ice and top with beer. Garnish with grapefruit and tears.

High Steaks

When I'm living out my final days, in a nursing home, dribbling and staring out the window, just hook me up to this cocktail and watch the toothless smile wash over my weathered face.

SERVES 6-8

150 g (5 oz) sliced capsicum (bell peppers)
400 ml (13½ fl oz) freshly squeezed lime juice
120 ml (4 fl oz) steak sauce
salt and freshly ground black pepper, to taste
1.5 litres (51 fl oz) chilled lager
lime, to garnish

In a large jug, muddle the capsicum with the lime juice, steak sauce and some salt and pepper.

Refrigerate overnight for the flavours to develop.

When ready to serve, carefully add the chilled lager to the capsicum mixture.

Pour into ice-filled glasses and garnish with lime.

Sex in a Canoe

The name says it all.

SERVES 1 DESIGNATED DRIVER

150 ml (5 fl oz) soda water (seltzer)
150 ml (5 fl oz) low-alcohol lager

Add the soda water to a tall
beer glass filled with ice.

Carefully top up with the 'beer'.

Garnish with a cocktail umbrella
and try not to go too crazy.

V-Plates

When I was 16, my friends and I would sneak into bars. We'd wear a shirt, trousers and dress shoes (so we'd look older), and we'd get there at 7.30 pm, before security started their shifts. We were such adults. Until we ordered this drink.

SERVES 1 MAN-CHILD

250 ml (8½ fl oz) lager
30 ml (1 fl oz) raspberry cordial

In the deepest voice you can muster from your pubescent mouth, ask an adult to pour the beer into a chilled beer glass.

Add the raspberry cordial.

Go nuts.

Flaming Dr. Pepper

This is not a drink for a quiet Sunday afternoon. This is one to have with a bunch of friends, when you're young and you don't have much money. Raid your parents' liquor cabinet for the amaretto and use the cheapest beer you can find.

SERVES 1

20 ml (¾ fl oz) amaretto

10 ml (¼ fl oz) 151 proof rum

375 ml (12½ fl oz) lager

Pour the amaretto into a shot glass.

Carefully float the rum on top by pouring it over the back of a metal spoon.

Pour the lager into a pint glass.

Using a match, light the rum. Stand around in a circle and intone some kind of douchebag chant, carefully drop the flaming shot glass into the pint glass and chug the contents.

Don't punch anyone.

Pales & Ales

Hard Shandy

This is the older, tougher brother to our lovable Shandy. He spent a few years on the inside and can drink whatever the hell he wants. I'm not going to tell him otherwise.

SERVES 1

45 ml (1½ fl oz) vodka

30 ml (1 fl oz) sugar syrup (page 9)

30 ml (1 fl oz) freshly squeezed lemon juice

40 ml (1¼ fl oz) chilled ginger beer

140 ml (4½ fl oz) IPA

mint sprig, to garnish

Combine the vodka, sugar syrup, lemon juice and ginger beer in a chilled beer glass.

Top up with the IPA.

Garnish with mint.

Bobby

In the olden days, people used to 'bob' for apples in a large barrel filled with ten gallons of beer that was fortified with apple brandy. The person who bobbed the last apple had to then drink the contents of the barrel and swim across the English Channel. This part may or may not be true.

SERVES 1

30 ml (1 fl oz) apple brandy
dash of bitters
10 ml (¼ fl oz) sugar syrup (page 9)
250 ml (8½ fl oz) Scotch ale
apple, to garnish

Combine the brandy, bitters and sugar syrup in a highball glass filled with ice.

Carefully add the beer. Garnish with apple.

Do not attempt to swim the English Channel.

Cascadian Caipirinha

Cachaça is the national drink of Brazil, made from distilled sugar cane juice. Its best mate is lime. Turns out, they're both pretty good friends with beer!

SERVES 1

1 lime, quartered
60 ml (2 fl oz) cachaça
15 ml (½ fl oz) agave syrup
330 ml (11 fl oz) bottle light-flavoured IPA

In a cocktail shaker, muddle the lime quarters.

Add the cachaça, agave syrup and 1 cup ice.

Shake like maracas.

Pour the contents into an old fashioned
glass and top with ice.

Carefully add the IPA.

Manhattan Brewski

The Manhattan is the martini of the whiskey world. This beerified version calls for a very strong, bitter IPA. You want something that can hold up to the flavour of the whiskey and not make the drink taste watered down.

SERVES 1

60 ml (2 fl oz) rye whiskey

30 ml (1 fl oz) sweet vermouth

30 ml (1 fl oz) strong-flavoured IPA

maraschino cherry, to garnish

Combine the whiskey and vermouth in a cocktail shaker filled with ice and stir.

Strain into a chilled martini glass and top with beer.

Garnish with a cherry.

Mendota

This cocktail is a bitter twist on the Mimosa. I repeat: this drink is bitter. It's for people with grown-up tastebuds. None of that childish lolly-water nonsense young whipper-snappers are drinking these days.

SERVES 1

330 ml (11 fl oz) bottle hoppy IPA or double IPA

90 ml (3 fl oz) freshly squeezed grapefruit juice

grapefruit twist, to garnish

Pour the beer into a chilled beer glass.

Add the grapefruit juice and
stir gently to combine.

Garnish with a twist of grapefruit rind.

Mixed Beeries

Belgian beers are often quite high in alcohol, sometimes giving them a sweetness that can work very well in cocktails. This one works well with Leffe Blonde or Duvel.

SERVES 1

4 raspberries
2 strawberries
6 blueberries
45 ml (1½ fl oz) gin
15 ml (½ fl oz) sugar syrup (page 9)
30 ml (1 fl oz) freshly squeezed lemon juice
60 ml (2 fl oz) chilled sweet Belgian ale
berries, to garnish

Muddle the berries in a cocktail shaker.

To the shaker, add the gin, sugar syrup and lemon juice. Shake vigorously.

Strain into a chilled martini glass and top with the beer.

Garnish with berries.

Monsalvat Mule

Drink this one in the snow, from a frosty copper cup.

SERVES 1

1 lime, quartered
5 mint leaves
30 ml (1 fl oz) bison grass vodka
15 ml (½ fl oz) ginger liqueur
330 ml (11 fl oz) bottle light-flavoured pale ale
mint sprigs, to garnish

Muddle the lime and mint leaves
in a cocktail shaker.

Add the vodka, ginger liqueur and 1 cup ice.

Shake vigorously, then pour the entire contents
into a copper cup or highball glass.

Add more ice and carefully top with beer.

Garnish with mint.

Bull's Eye

This drink comes all the way from Cuba, the land of sunshine, moonshine, rum, cigars, Che Guevara T-shirts and communists.

80 ml (2½ fl oz) freshly squeezed lime juice

330 ml (11 fl oz) bottle pale ale

200 ml (7 fl oz) ginger beer

1–2 teaspoons sugar

mint, to garnish

Add the lime juice to a chilled pint glass filled with crushed ice.

Slowly add the pale ale and ginger beer.

Stir in sugar to taste.

Garnish with mint.

Smoky Beer Sangrita

Sangrita is a spicy, citrusy concoction that is traditionally used as a companion to straight tequila. If you've never had good tequila with sangrita, you should really seek it out. It's salty, spicy and sour, and really plays off with the smokiness of tequila. My mouth is literally watering as I write this. But enough about tequila, this book is about beer. This cocktail brings the savoury awesomeness of sangrita and drops it straight into an icy cold beer.

SERVES 1–8

½ teaspoon harissa

250 ml (8½ fl oz) tomato juice

180 ml (6 fl oz) freshly squeezed grapefruit juice

120 ml (4 fl oz) freshly squeezed orange juice

45 ml (1½ fl oz) freshly squeezed lemon juice

60 ml (2 fl oz) freshly squeezed lime juice

¼ teaspoon freshly ground black pepper

120 ml (4 fl oz) hoppy IPA

grapefruit wedges and smoked salt, to garnish

To make the sangrita, combine the harissa,
tomato juice and citrus juices in a jug. Add
the black pepper and stir vigorously.

Refrigerate for 4 hours to let the flavours develop.

To serve, rim highball glasses with
grapefruit and smoked salt.

Fill with ice and add 120 ml (4 fl oz)
sangrita to each glass.

Carefully top with beer and garnish
with a grapefruit wedge.

Camparipa

I like to drink a Negroni before dinner, but they do tend to be quite high in alcohol, which can lead to adverse health effects like arguing with a loved one or trampling on a pet. This bitter little mistress is a great aperitif that cleanses the palate but keeps the head clear before a gastronomic adventure.

SERVES 2

---

60 ml (2 fl oz) Campari

---

330 ml (11 fl oz) bottle IPA

---

250 ml (8½ fl oz) sparkling blood orange juice

---

orange, to garnish

Divide the Campari between two
old fashioned glasses filled with ice.

Top up with the IPA, then the blood orange juice.

Garnish with orange.

Take care of yourself, and each other.

Hammered Scotsman

The Scottish are a hard people. This short little red-headed Scotsman will punch you in the chin if you're not careful.

SERVES 1

30 ml (1 fl oz) Scotch whisky
30 ml (1 fl oz) Drambuie
30 ml (1 fl oz) Scottish red ale

Pour the whisky and Drambuie into an old fashioned glass filled with ice.

Add the beer and stir with a rusty nail.

Pineapple Hop

This cocktail calls for an ingredient called pineapple shrub. Shrub is a flavoured drinking vinegar that is becoming increasingly popular among bartenders, as it adds a more complex acidity to drinks than your standard lemon or lime juice. Pineapple shrub works well with heavily hopped beers, as it complements the 'pineapple notes' found in the beer.

SERVES 4–8

1 pineapple, peeled and cut into cubes
330 g (11½ oz/1½ cups) sugar
375 ml (12½ fl oz) apple cider vinegar
150 ml (5 fl oz) white rum
35 ml (1¼ fl oz) orgeat syrup (almond syrup)
600 ml (20½ fl oz) chilled IPA
cherries, to garnish

To make the shrub, muddle the pineapple chunks with the sugar in a large container.

Refrigerate overnight.

Strain the liquid into a sterilised jar. You can discard or eat the pineapple flesh.

Add the vinegar and seal the jar. Refrigerate for 2 weeks, shaking the jar every second day.

After 2 weeks, strain the liquid into a clean, airtight container. The shrub will keep refrigerated for up to 6 months.

In a large jug, combine the rum, orgeat syrup and 150 ml (5 fl oz) of the shrub. Refrigerate for 2 hours, or up to 24 hours.

When ready to serve, slowly add the beer to the jug and gently stir to combine.

Pour into small glasses filled with ice and garnish with cherries.

Ping Pong Punch

This is a very simple punch that will kickstart your next backyard barbecue. Try it with beer pong. Nobody will win.

SERVES 6–12

---

600 ml (20½ fl oz) chilled pineapple juice

180 ml (6 fl oz) chilled yellow Chartreuse

6 x 330 ml (11 fl oz) chilled bottles amber ale

In a large punch bowl, combine the pineapple juice and Chartreuse.

Slowly add the beer.

Garnish with ping pong balls.

British Colonialism

Some people think that IPA (or India Pale Ale) comes from India, when in fact it was English ale made stronger and with more hops so that it would survive the long boat journey from Britain to India. The alpha acids in the hops that give the beer its refreshing bitterness also act as a preserving agent. Back in those days it was safer to drink 6.5% beer and steer a ship than it was to drink the water.

SERVES 1

45 ml (1½ fl oz) dry gin
10 ml (¼ fl oz) elderflower liqueur
90 ml (3 fl oz) grapefruit juice
330 ml (11 fl oz) bottle IPA
grapefruit twist, to garnish

In a cocktail shaker filled with ice,
combine the gin, liqueur and grapefruit
juice and shake vigorously.

Strain into an old fashioned glass filled with ice.

Top with the IPA and garnish with
a twist of grapefruit rind.

Depth Charge

In the old days, a depth charge was an anti-submarine weapon that was dropped into the ocean to blow up naughty people. This liquid version seems to be just as destructive, making you do things you would never tell your mother about. You can use any spirit or liqueur in this, but for demonstration I'm using vodka.

SERVES 1

330 ml (11 fl oz) bottle pale ale
30 ml (1 fl oz) vodka

Carefully pour the beer into a pint glass.

Pour the vodka into a shot glass.

Drop the shot glass into the pint glass and chug the entire contents.

Call your mother.

Rue de Barbara

Here's a drink you can curl up into after dinner. The rich maltiness of the Scotch ale marries wonderfully with the tartness of the rhubarb, and the pisco just warms you from the inside.

SERVES 1

220 g (8 oz/1 cup) sugar
125 g (4½ oz/1 cup) sliced rhubarb
1 vanilla bean, cut in half lengthways, plus an extra to garnish
45 ml (1½ fl oz) pisco
90 ml (3 fl oz) Scotch ale

Combine the sugar, rhubarb and vanilla bean
in a saucepan. Add 125 ml (4 fl oz) water and
bring to the boil over medium–high heat.

Reduce the heat to low and simmer for 10 minutes.

Remove from the heat and allow
to stand for 30 minutes.

Strain into a clean, airtight jar and
refrigerate. The rhubarb syrup will keep
in the fridge for up to 2 weeks.

When ready to serve, fill an
old fashioned glass with ice.

Add the pisco and 30 ml (1 fl oz)
of the rhubarb syrup.

Carefully top up with the beer
and gently stir to combine.

Garnish with a vanilla bean.

Cerveza Amanecer

Here we have a beery, bitter and, in my opinion, better version of the tequila sunrise. Much more complex flavours going on here than just tequila, orange juice and cordial.

SERVES 1

45 ml (1½ fl oz) silver tequila
2 dashes orange bitters
75 ml (2½ fl oz) freshly squeezed orange juice
15 ml (½ fl oz) maraschino liqueur
330 ml (11 fl oz) bottle double IPA
orange and maraschino cherry, to garnish

In a cocktail shaker filled with ice, combine the tequila, bitters and orange juice. Shake like maracas.

Strain into a tall beer glass filled with ice. Add the maraschino liqueur, then carefully top up with the beer.

Garnish with orange and a cherry.

Cool Hand Cuke

It's hard to stop at just one of these refreshing cocktails. But surely no man can drink 50 of them?

SERVES 1

45 ml (1½ fl oz) vodka
2 basil leaves, chopped
¼ cucumber, sliced, plus extra to garnish
30 ml (1 fl oz) agave syrup
90 ml (3 fl oz) chilled soda water (seltzer)
120 ml (4 fl oz) good, citrusy IPA
basil leaves, to garnish

In a cocktail shaker filled with ice, combine the vodka, basil, cucumber and agave syrup. Shake vigorously.

Strain into a tall, chilled beer glass.

Add the soda water and stir to combine.

Slowly add the beer.

Garnish with cucumber and basil leaves.

Bitter Rivals

Bitter on bitter with bitters. Sweet!

SERVES 1

60 ml (2 fl oz) Campari
330 ml (11 fl oz) bottle IPA
dash of orange bitters
orange twist, to garnish

Pour the Campari into an old fashioned
glass and fill with ice.

Carefully add the beer.

Splash the bitters on top and garnish
with a twist of orange rind.

Beggar's Banquet

Sweet and warming, like a nice fire in a
44-gallon drum on a cold winter's night, here's
a sipper for when you're wearing slippers.

SERVES 1

60 ml (2 fl oz) bourbon
10 ml (¼ fl oz) freshly squeezed lemon juice
20 ml (¾ fl oz) maple syrup
2 dashes bitters
150 ml (5 fl oz) English red ale
orange, to garnish

In a cocktail shaker filled with ice, combine the
bourbon, lemon juice, maple syrup and bitters.

Shake vigorously, then strain into
a tall glass filled with ice.

Top with the beer and garnish with orange.

Saisons, Sours, Weizens & Wildcards

Beerlini

This slender little take on the Italian breakfast drink doesn't leave you with acid reflux and heartburn. Also, it's better because it's got beer in it.

30 ml (1 fl oz) peach nectar
100 ml (3½ fl oz) wheat beer
strawberry, to garnish

Add the peach nectar to a chilled champagne flute.

Slowly top up with the beer.

Garnish with a strawberry.

Blood Orange Shandy

Blood oranges are such a vibrant-looking fruit, with a refreshing bitterness. Next time they're in season, grab a bag and a six-pack of hefeweizen and whip up this baby. The almond extract really brings this drink to life, but you only need the tiniest amount.

SERVES 1

330 ml (11 fl oz) bottle hefeweizen

1 blood orange, juiced, plus extra to garnish

1 drop almond extract

Pour the beer into a chilled, short glass. Add the orange juice.

Add the almond extract and garnish with blood orange.

Raspberry Snake Bite

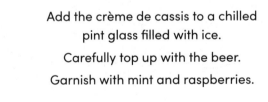

Lambic beer is made using wild yeast found in Belgium's Zenne Valley. This wild yeast creates a very interesting sour flavour in the beer. Personally, it is my favourite kind of beer, but it's not to everyone's taste. Either way, it's less hoppy than traditional ales and a lot easier to use in cocktails. Next time you're in your local craft beer shop, find a bottle and open your mind to a whole new world of beer drinking.

SERVES 1

30 ml (1 fl oz) crème de cassis
330 ml (11 fl oz) bottle raspberry lambic
mint and raspberries, to garnish

Add the crème de cassis to a chilled pint glass filled with ice.

Carefully top up with the beer.

Garnish with mint and raspberries.

Brass Monkey

Made famous by the Beastie Boys in 1986, this is a very simple drink designed to achieve maximum drunkenness at the lowest possible price, without making you go blind. It uses malt liquor, which is a very strong, very cheap beer found mainly in North America. You could replace it with a strong Belgian Trappist ale, but that would be an insult to the monks.

SERVES 1-5

1180 ml (40 fl oz) bottle malt liquor
350 ml (12 fl oz) orange juice

Open the bottle of malt liquor and drink it until the level reaches the top of the label.

Carefully add the orange juice.

Replace the cap and slowly tip the bottle upside down to combine the ingredients, being careful not to cover oneself in malt liquor.

Take an old-school ghetto blaster, crank the Beastie Boys' *Licensed to Ill* up to 11 and intimidate some of the older generations at your local park.

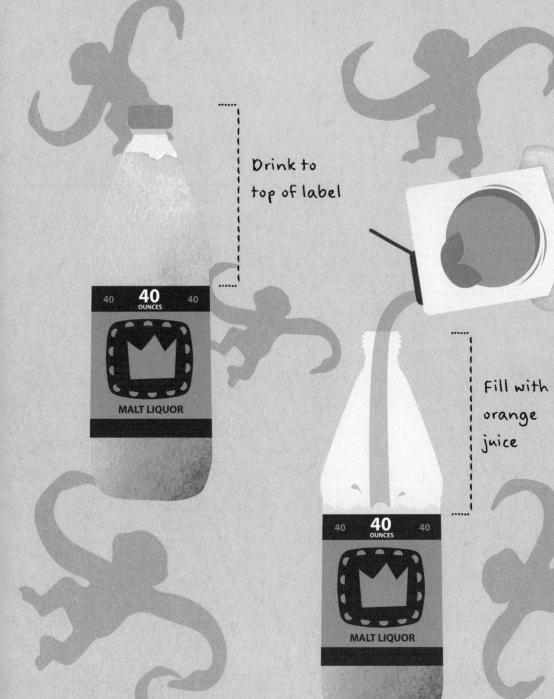

Ginger Rum Shandy

It's always difficult to find a drink that goes well with spicy food. Wheat beer is always a great match. Try this spicy little number next time you're eating Thai food.

SERVES 4

2 cm (¾ inch) piece fresh ginger, peeled and sliced
220 g (8 oz/1 cup) sugar
120 ml (4 fl oz) spiced rum
60 ml (2 fl oz) freshly squeezed lime juice
60 ml (2 fl oz) cloudy apple juice
500 ml (17 fl oz) wheat beer
apple and grated ginger, to garnish

In a saucepan, combine the ginger and sugar. Add 250 ml (8½ fl oz) water and place over medium–high heat. Bring to the boil, then reduce the heat to low. Allow to simmer for 10–15 minutes, stirring occasionally, until the mixture reaches a syrupy consistency.

Remove from the heat, then strain and chill.

In a cocktail shaker filled with ice, combine 1 tablespoon of the ginger syrup, 30 ml (1 fl oz) of the rum, 15 ml (½ fl oz) of the lime juice, and 15 ml (½ fl oz) of the apple juice.

Shake, then strain into an old fashioned glass filled with ice.

Repeat with the remaining ingredients, until you have four glasses.

Top each glass with wheat beer.

Garnish with apple and grated ginger.

Brewgria

A hot summer's day, barbecue in the backyard, relaxing with friends and family: it's days like these you need a nice punch in your throat to quench that hard-earned thirst. This take on the classic Spanish sangria is a little lower in alcohol so you can drink twice as much.

SERVES 6-8

1 apple, sliced
1 orange, sliced
1 lemon, sliced
10 strawberries, sliced
4 x 330 ml (11 fl oz) bottles fruity wheat beer
2 x 330 ml (11 fl oz) bottles raspberry lambic
500 ml (17 fl oz) ginger beer

In a large punchbowl, carefully combine all the ingredients, without frothing up the beer too much.

Add large blocks of ice. Chill.

Sporty, Posh, Ginger, Baby

I'll tell you what I want, what I really, really want: a tastebud tingling, tantalising tipple to tide me over. This one is sexy, svelte and sophisticated, with just enough trash-bag to still be a lot of fun.

SERVES 1

30 ml (1 fl oz) vodka

15 ml (½ fl oz) ginger liqueur

30 ml (1 fl oz) freshly squeezed lemon juice

100 ml (3½ fl oz) Berliner Weisse or wheat beer

candied ginger, to garnish

Combine the vodka, liqueur and lemon juice in a cocktail shaker filled with ice and shake vigorously.

Strain into a chilled martini glass.

Top with the beer and garnish with candied ginger.

Of Her Own Accord

Slight hints of tropical flavours, without being a tacky tiki cocktail.

SERVES 1

30 ml (1 fl oz) amontillado sherry
15 ml (½ fl oz) Jamaican rum
10 ml (¼ fl oz) banana liqueur
15 ml (½ fl oz) freshly squeezed lemon juice
60 ml (2 fl oz) Berliner Weisse or wheat beer
mint, to garnish

Combine the sherry, rum, liqueur and lemon juice in a cocktail shaker filled with ice.

Shake, then stain into a highball glass filled with crushed ice.

Slowly add the beer.

Garnish with mint.

Sweet Blonde

Blondes have more fun, right? Well this sassy little number has two blondes in cider ... how much fun does that sound? There are many blondes to try, so don't stop at the first one you come across.

SERVES 4

330 ml (11 fl oz) bottle blonde wheat beer

330 ml (11 fl oz) bottle blonde ale

330 ml (11 fl oz) bottle cider

Evenly distribute the wheat beer among four chilled glasses.

Add the blonde ale to each glass.

Top each one off with cider.

Remember to be a gentleman.

Sidewalker

Here's a punch for people with a sweet tooth. Interestingly, this drink is balanced with the addition of apple cider vinegar. It's sweet, sour and alcoholic – much like my beloved grandma. Drink the whole jug yourself and you'll find out where the name comes from.

SERVES 4-8

180 ml (6 fl oz) maple syrup
90 ml (3 fl oz) apple cider vinegar
300 ml (10 fl oz) freshly squeezed lemon juice
300 ml (10 fl oz) applejack or apple brandy
3 x 330 ml (11 fl oz) bottles hefeweizen
200 ml (7 fl oz) soda water (seltzer)
apple, to garnish

In a large jug, combine the maple syrup,
vinegar, lemon juice and apple brandy.

Fill with ice and chill.

Carefully add the beer and soda
water. Stir to combine.

Pour into highball or beer glasses filled
with ice and garnish with apple.

Beer Hive

Here's an after-dinner cocktail that could really hold its own with a cheese platter. Beer is often a better pairing with cheese than wine. Here the honey adds a touch of sweetness that lends itself to sharper, saltier cheeses, while the gin gives the alcoholic kick you want in a cocktail.

SERVES 1

15 ml (½ fl oz) honey
45 ml (1½ fl oz) gin
30 ml (1 fl oz) freshly squeezed lemon juice
90 ml (3 fl oz) hefeweizen
lemon, to garnish

Dissolve the honey in 15 ml (½ fl oz) water to make 30 ml (1 fl oz) of honey syrup. Add the syrup to a cocktail shaker filled with ice. Add the gin and lemon juice.

Shake vigorously, then strain into a tall glass filled with ice.

Top with beer and garnish with lemon.

Fiery Blonde

Beer goes so very well with hot, spicy food. Some people even like to put hot, spicy food into their beer! This is the drink for them.

SERVES 1

330 ml (11 fl oz) bottle blonde ale or wheat beer

80 ml (2½ fl oz) freshly squeezed lime juice

2½ teaspoons sugar

¼ teaspoon sea salt, plus extra to taste

¼ teaspoon chilli powder, plus extra to taste

lime, to garnish

Slowly pour the beer into a short glass filled with ice.

Add the lime juice, sugar, salt and chilli powder and stir to combine.

Garnish with lime, and add more salt and/or chilli to your liking.

Aperol Mist

Aperol is a rhubarb liqueur and a fantastic addition to anyone's bar. You can mix it with gin, vodka, wine, soda, and now, beer.

SERVES 1

45 ml (1½ fl oz) Aperol

30 ml (1 fl oz) freshly squeezed lemon juice

330 ml (11 fl oz) bottle witbier (Belgian wheat beer)

lemon twist, to garnish

Combine the Aperol and lemon juice in a chilled pint glass filled with ice.

Carefully top up with beer.

Garnish with a twist of lemon rind.

Summer Hoedown

Once you finish this punch you can wear the watermelon on your head and run around the backyard with your pants down.

1 watermelon, hollowed out, flesh diced
2 tablespoons sugar
60 ml (2 fl oz) maraschino liqueur
4 x 330 ml (11 fl oz) bottles witbier (Belgian wheat beer)
mint, to garnish

In batches, blend the watermelon flesh until smooth. Strain the watermelon juice through a fine-mesh strainer and discard the pulp.

Stir the sugar and liqueur into the watermelon juice and refrigerate until chilled.

Pour the chilled mixture into a large jug (or into the watermelon) with large blocks of ice and carefully top up with beer.

Garnish with mint.

Deflorer

A delightful summery punch to share among friends,
or with people you want to become friends with.

SERVES 6–9

---

90 ml (3 fl oz) freshly squeezed pink
grapefruit juice

---

90 ml (3 fl oz) freshly squeezed lemon juice

---

180 ml (6 fl oz) chilled gin

---

140 ml (4½ fl oz) chilled elderflower liqueur

---

20 ml (¾ fl oz) sugar syrup (page 9)

---

3 dashes orange bitters

---

6 x 330 ml (11 fl oz) chilled bottles
wheat beer

---

grapefruit twists, to garnish

In a very large jug or punch bowl, combine the
fruit juices, gin, liqueur, sugar syrup and bitters.

Slowly add the beer. Serve immediately,
garnished with twists of grapefruit rind.

110

Harvey Weissbanger

You know how there's always been that tall skinny bottle of Galliano sitting in the corner of your liquor cabinet because nobody seems to drink it? Here's a recipe that will slowly work it down. Who knows, you might like it so much you find yourself buying another one ...

SERVES 1

---

30 ml (1 fl oz) Galliano L'Autentico

---

60 ml (2 fl oz) freshly squeezed orange juice

---

330 ml (11 fl oz) bottle wheat beer

---

orange wheel, to garnish

In a tall glass filled with ice, combine
the Galliano and orange juice.

Carefully top up with beer.

Garnish with an orange wheel.

The Bitter End

There are quite a lot of flavoured fruit beers available today. Craft brewers are going to great lengths to find a style of beer that is truly original. While interesting, they're not always amazing – so if you end up with a fruit beer you don't particularly like, try mixing it into a cocktail!

SERVES 1

30 ml (1 fl oz) white rum

1½ teaspoons freshly squeezed lemon juice

1 blood orange, juiced, plus extra to garnish

180 ml (6 fl oz) grapefruit beer

grapefruit, to garnish

In a chilled beer glass, combine the rum, lemon juice and orange juice.

Fill with ice, then carefully add the beer. Gently stir to combine.

Garnish with grapefruit and blood orange.

Bananenweizen

When you need a little pick-me-up, this cocktail will really put the bananen back in your weizen.

SERVES 1

500 ml (17 fl oz) chilled weissbier
(German wheat beer)

60 ml (2 fl oz) chilled banana juice

Carefully pour the beer into a chilled pint glass.

Add the banana juice.

Stir and enjoy.

Weizen Sour

Here's a delicious take on a whisky sour. Try to find a nice wheat beer with spicy orange-rind notes, such as Hoegaarden, to play off with the marmalade.

SERVES 1

60 ml (2 fl oz) bourbon
20 ml (¾ fl oz) freshly squeezed lemon juice
15 ml (½ fl oz) sugar syrup (page 9)
½ tablespoon orange marmalade
2 dashes orange bitters
60 ml (2 fl oz) weissbier (German wheat beer)
lemon twist, to garnish

In a cocktail shaker filled with ice, combine
the bourbon, lemon juice, sugar syrup,
marmalade and bitters. Shake vigorously.

Strain into an old fashioned glass filled with ice.

Top up with beer and garnish
with a twist of lemon rind.

Honeydew Hefe

The Honeydew Hefe is the perfect post-workout smoothie. Full of electrolytes, protein, omega-3s and antioxidants, it truly is a superfood. Just kidding – it's beer and ice cream!

SERVES 1-3

½ honeydew melon, peeled and cut into chunks, plus extra to garnish

3 cups vanilla ice cream

250 ml (8½ fl oz) hefeweizen

½ teaspoon vanilla extract

Place half the honeydew chunks in the freezer for 1 hour.

Combine all the remaining ingredients (except the garnish) in a blender.

Blend at high speed until smooth.

Pour into milkshake glasses and garnish with honeydew.

Stouts, Porters & other dark beers

Black Russian Imperial

Russian imperial stout is high in alcohol and rich in flavour. If you can find one that has been infused with coffee as well, you're on your way to a great end to the night. Be careful, this cocktail gets you behind the eyes like an ice pick to the back of the head.

SERVES 1

---
45 ml (1½ fl oz) Russian vodka
---
60 ml (2 fl oz) Russian imperial stout
---
maraschino cherry, to garnish

Pour the vodka into an old fashioned glass filled with ice.

Carefully add the stout.

Garnish with a cherry, skewered onto a miniature ice pick.

Black & Tan

Blending beers can make the heavier, more alcoholic stouts more sessionable. Experiment with combining different flavours.

SERVES 1

285 ml (9½ fl oz) stout
285 ml (9½ fl oz) pale ale

Combine the beers in a chilled pint glass.

Hangman's Blood

The Long Island Iced Tea of beer cocktails.
This is not for the faint-hearted. Do not operate
heavy machinery after one of these.

SERVES 1

30 ml (1 fl oz) gin
30 ml (1 fl oz) rum
30 ml (1 fl oz) Irish whiskey
30 ml (1 fl oz) brandy
30 ml (1 fl oz) tawny port
120 ml (4 fl oz) sparkling wine
150 ml (5 fl oz) porter

Combine the spirits and port in a
chilled pint glass with ½ cup of ice.

Add the sparkling wine and porter.

Black Velvet

This drink dates back to 1861, when it was invented to mourn the death of Prince Albert, husband of Queen Victoria. It is best made with Guinness and a sweeter sparkling wine.

SERVES 1

---

120 ml (4 fl oz) sparkling wine

---

60 ml (2 fl oz) stout

Add the sparkling wine to a chilled champagne flute.

Top with the stout.

Irish Manhattan

The island of Manhattan has rich Irish roots. This drink is a tip of the tweed flat cap to that history.

SERVES 1

45 ml (1½ fl oz) Irish whiskey
20 ml (¾ fl oz) sweet vermouth
2 dashes bitters
440 ml (15 fl oz) can Guinness

In a cocktail shaker filled with ice, combine the whiskey, vermouth and bitters. Stir, then strain into a chilled martini glass.

Into a separate pint glass, pour out the entire can of Guinness. Allow to settle.

Scoop the creamy foam into the martini glass.

Winter Warmer

This lovely winter warmer would be perfect at Christmas time for those who live on the top half of the planet. It also makes good use of all those broken candy canes lying around after the festive season. If you can find a nitrogen-infused milk stout, it will make for a delightfully creamy concoction.

SERVES 1

4 candy canes, broken, plus
1 extra to garnish

700 ml (23½ fl oz) bottle coffee liqueur

500 ml (17 fl oz) bottle milk stout

At least two days before, add the broken candy canes to the bottle of coffee liqueur. Shake every now and then to infuse the flavour.

Strain the coffee liqueur and discard any leftover candy cane. Return the liqueur to its original bottle. You now have candy cane-infused coffee liqueur.

To serve, pour 60 ml (2 fl oz) of the liqueur into a chilled pint glass.

Carefully add the stout.

Garnish with a candy cane and have a merry Christmas.

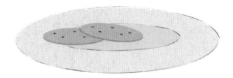

Coffee Stout Espresso Martini

An evening tipple for the metrosexual beer drinker.

SERVES 1

30 ml (1 fl oz) silver tequila
15 ml (½ fl oz) agave syrup
30 ml (1 fl oz) chilled espresso coffee
5 ml (1/8 fl oz) vanilla extract
45 ml (1½ fl oz) coffee milk stout
coffee beans and a vanilla bean, to garnish

Fill a cocktail shaker with ice.
Add the tequila, agave syrup, coffee
and vanilla extract. Shake vigorously.

Strain into a chilled martini glass,
then top with the stout.

Garnish with coffee and vanilla beans.

Smoke Stack

Now that it's punishable by death to smoke in or near a restaurant, we've had to find other ways to make our mouths taste like an ashtray. This cocktail is like drinking a nice cigar.

SERVES 1

30 ml (1 fl oz) smoky Scotch whisky
250 ml (8½ fl oz) smoked porter
250 ml (8½ fl oz) Scotch ale
tobacco leaf, to garnish

Pour the whisky into a chilled pint glass.

Carefully add the porter, then the ale.

Garnish with a tobacco leaf.

Dublin Iced Coffee

Here's a little pick-me-up for a sunny Sunday morning. It works best with a coffee stout or porter, but for authenticity you could easily use Guinness and you'd be just as happy.

SERVES 1

45 ml (1½ fl oz) Irish whiskey
20 ml (¾ fl oz) sugar syrup (page 9)
60 ml (2 fl oz) coffee stout or porter
60 ml (2 fl oz) cold-brew coffee
15 ml (½ fl oz) cream
cinnamon stick, for grating

Fill a tall, chilled beer glass with ice.
Add the whiskey, sugar syrup, beer and coffee. Gently stir to combine.

Layer the cream on top of the cocktail by slowly pouring it over the back of a metal spoon.

Finely grate some cinnamon on top to garnish.

Brown Nuts Float

When you've had a lovely dinner and you want some ice cream but you also want a beer, the only thing to do is combine the two. There are many chocolate stouts and porters in the craft beer market now; a sweet, syrupy number works best here. Experiment with a few different types.

SERVES 1

1 scoop vanilla ice cream
30 ml (1 fl oz) hazelnut liqueur
330 ml (11 fl oz) bottle chocolate stout or porter
chilled dark chocolate, for grating

Add the ice cream and liqueur to a pint glass.

Very carefully and slowly, pour the beer over the top.

Garnish with grated chocolate.

Brown Town

Here's a beery take on the classic Old Fashioned.
In my experience, this cocktail is the only
acceptable use of Southern Comfort.

SERVES 1

60 ml (2 fl oz) brown ale
30 ml (1 fl oz) bourbon
1 teaspoon Southern Comfort
10 ml (¼ fl oz) maple syrup
maraschino cherry, to garnish

Add the beer, bourbon, Southern Comfort
and maple syrup to a cocktail shaker
filled with ice. Gently stir to combine.

Strain into a chilled old fashioned glass.

Garnish with a cherry.

Stout Diplomat

This cocktail gets its name from the Venezuelan rum Ron Diplomático. You can use any aged rum, but not one that is too spiced or you'll overpower the delicious beer. Remember, it's all about the beer.

SERVES 1

30 ml (1 fl oz) aged rum
15 ml (½ fl oz) Pedro Ximénez sherry
180 ml (6 fl oz) chocolate stout

Combine the rum and sherry
in a chilled beer glass.

Slowly add the stout.

Grab your finest patent leather attaché
case and try not to start any arguments.

Stout Flip

We've seen beer cocktails you can drink with
breakfast – here's one you can drink *for* breakfast.
It works best with a nice creamy oatmeal stout.

SERVES 1

60 ml (2 fl oz) Averna
30 ml (1 fl oz) oatmeal stout
2 dashes bitters
1 egg
whole nutmeg, for grating

Fill a cocktail shaker with ice. Add the Averna,
stout, bitters and egg, and shake vigorously.

Strain into a chilled wine glass or martini glass.

Finely grate nutmeg on top to garnish.

Ruddy Mary

Here's one for when you want a more savoury edge to your beer. To add a kick, use half tomato juice, half vodka.

SERVES 1

330 ml (11 fl oz) bottle English dark ale
30 ml (1 fl oz) tomato juice
dash of hot sauce
celery, to garnish

Pour the beer into a chilled pint glass. Add the tomato juice.

Season with hot sauce to taste. Garnish with celery.

Black Forest Cake

A delightfully dark and delicious dessert drink,
with flavours of bitter chocolate and sour cherries.

SERVES 1

30 ml (1 fl oz) chilled raspberry lambic
45 ml (1½ fl oz) chilled chocolate porter
15 ml (½ fl oz) chilled maraschino liqueur
10 ml (¼ fl oz) chilled amaretto
30 ml (1 fl oz) cream
maraschino cherry, to garnish

Add the beers and liqueurs to an
old fashioned glass filled with ice.

Add the cream to a cocktail shaker
filled with ice and shake vigorously.

Layer the cream on top of the cocktail by slowly
pouring it over the back of a metal spoon.

Garnish with a cherry.

Chocolate Cookie

Who doesn't love a good chocolate cookie?
This is the kind of cookie parents bring out
after the kids go to bed. Keep well away from
children. That's just a general rule for life.

SERVES 1

30 ml (1 fl oz) chilled cinnamon liqueur
30 ml (1 fl oz) chilled Scotch ale
30 ml (1 fl oz) chilled chocolate porter
whole nutmeg, for grating

Pour the liqueur into a chilled martini glass.

Slowly add the ale, then the porter.

Finely grate nutmeg on top to garnish.

Terry's

Every year for Christmas I used to get a
Terry's Chocolate Orange. Here's the version
I enjoy at Christmas time these days.

SERVES 1

330 ml (11 fl oz) bottle chocolate porter
45 ml (1½ fl oz) Grand Marnier

Pour the porter into a chilled beer glass.

Add the Grand Marnier.

Don't stir.

Bitter Pumpkin

Here's a Halloween cocktail to sip while sitting on your porch in your rocking chair, nursing a shotgun and telling kids to get off your lawn.

30 ml (1 fl oz) rye whiskey	
15 ml (½ fl oz) Averna	
10 ml (¼ fl oz) lemon juice	
10 ml (¼ fl oz) sugar syrup (page 9)	
1 tablespoon pumpkin butter	
2 dashes bitters	
330 ml (11 fl oz) bottle dark ale	
lemon, to garnish	

Fill a cocktail shaker with ice. Add the whiskey, Averna, lemon juice, sugar syrup, pumpkin butter and bitters. Shake vigorously and strain into an old fashioned glass, with one large ice cube.

Carefully top with beer. Garnish with lemon.

Guinness Creamy Soda

An adult version of a childhood classic. Grab two straws, drop a dime in the jukebox and party like it's 1959.

SERVES 2

90 ml (3 fl oz) chilled ginger liqueur
90 ml (3 fl oz) chilled vanilla liqueur
90 ml (3 fl oz) chilled soda water (seltzer)
90 ml (3 fl oz) chilled Guinness
whipped cream and maraschino cherry, to garnish

In a chilled milkshake glass, combine the liqueurs and soda water. Stir gently.

Slowly add the Guinness.

Insert two straws, top with whipped cream and pop a cherry on top.

Remember kids: if it's not on, it's not on.

Index

Published in 2017 by Smith Street Books
Melbourne | Australia
smithstreetbooks.com

ISBN: 978-1-925418-43-9

CIP data is available from the National Library of Australia.

Publisher: Paul McNally
Project editor: Hannah Koelmeyer
Editor: Katri Hilden
Design: Kate Barraclough
Illustration and layout: Dave Adams

Printed & bound in China by C&C Offset Printing Co., Ltd.

Book 35
10 9 8 7 6 5 4 3 2 1